The Selected ROY McFADDEN

The Selected ROY MCFADDEN

edited by John Boyd

The Blackstaff Press

British Library Cataloguing in Publication Data

McFadden, Roy
  The selected Roy McFadden
  I. Title   II. Boyd, John, 19--
  821'.914   PR6063.C
  ISBN 0-85640-282-6

First published in 1983

© Introduction, John Boyd 1983
© Poems, Roy McFadden 1983
© This selection, The Blackstaff Press 1983

Published by The Blackstaff Press Limited
3 Galway Park, Dundonald BT16 0AN
with the assistance of
The Arts Council of Northern Ireland

All rights reserved

Printed in Northern Ireland by Belfast Litho Printers

for Margaret

For Margaret

Contents

Introduction   1
    Prefatory Poem   7

Translations and Reiterations
    Jonathan Swift   11
    Lines by Slieve Donard   12
    Dublin to Belfast: wartime   13
    The drums   14
    Lines written near Downpatrick after an air-raid   15
    Homecoming   16
    Prophet and loss   17
    Liverpool boat   18
    Elegy for a sixth-former   19
    Paul Robeson   20
    Elegy for a noncombatant   21
    Portrait of a poet   23
    Elegy for a dog   24
    Death of a cyclist   25
    My father had a clock   26
    The white bird   27
    The upland field   28
    First letter to an Irish novelist   31

The Garryowen
    The Arcadia   37
    Glenarm   38
    Independence   39
    Brendan Behan   40
    Roger Casement's Rising   41
    Sheepdog trials   42
    Synge in Paris   43
    Folkminder   44
    Night fishing   45
    Premonition   46

Second letter to an Irish novelist	47
Contemplations of Mary	49
The Garryowen	53

Verifications
March	59
Keeping my place	60
Kew Gardens	63
Daisymount Terrace	65
Irish Chippendale	67
The lay preacher	68
Tuesday	69

A Watching Brief
Out in the country	73
Overtime	75
Self-generation	76
Allotments	77
Armistice Day 1938	78
Sound sense	79

Notes for the Hinterland
Post-war	83
The Grand Central Hotel	84
Conveyancer	87
Mortgage redemptions	88
Sancto's dog	89
Time's present	92
Helston	93
After the broadcast	94
Maryville Street	95
Sketches of Boz	96

Bibliography   103

Introduction

There are of course various approaches to the work of any poet. My own approach to Roy McFadden's poems is personal. By that I mean that I have shared in the enjoyment of many of the poems with the poet himself, listened to private readings of them, discussed them, and on one or two occasions inspired a stanza.

A poet, like a dramatist, frequently makes such use of his friends, and my friendship with McFadden has lasted almost a lifetime.

Consequently I cannot and have no wish to claim impartiality. On the contrary I claim partiality. I have been reading his work throughout the period of our long friendship, and still look forward to a new poem as eagerly as I did when the poet as a young man walked the winding country road from Lisburn to my home in the village of Ballymacash, from where I was editing *Lagan*. This periodical – a bold venture in its day – is long forgotten, lying on the shelves of a few writers and in a few libraries. Many of its contributors are dead; some have given up writing in despair; only a handful have endured. McFadden has not only endured but has long been one of Ireland's most distinguished poets. This selection is overdue.

But let me frankly confess to a mild prejudice against 'selections'. Admittedly they are useful appetisers, especially if the whole work is not readily available, which is the case with McFadden. But a 'selection' should serve the limited purpose of being only a prelude to appreciation of the whole work: never to be used as an excuse for postponing the 'collected'.

To write an introduction to a poet's work is to risk the accusation of puffery. To puff is to overpraise: and to overpraise is to invite scepticism. And a reader properly resents having his own judgment cavalierly pre-empted. Besides, McFadden himself, a most fastidious man, has always looked askance at publicity. For example, commenting on some contemporary poets in 'Self-Generation':

> Their singular self-esteem, he said, aggrieved,
> Upstages poetry
> With cult of personality;
> The nipple-greed to be the best-beloved,
> Exclusively.

Poetry is more a private than a public art, and a poet more a private person than a self-publicist. To display one's wares at the drop of a cheque is all too often to devalue the currency of the poetic word.

Roy McFadden was born in Belfast on 14 November 1921, the second son of Roland Victor McFadden, a bank official whose family came from Downpatrick, and Maud Steel, whose family came from County Durham.

I quote an autobiographical essay published in *Threshold* (1975), not only to give a vignette of his childhood but to exemplify the wit and vigour of his prose:

> I was born, the certificate informs on me, in Beechfield Street. I didn't presume there very long, for the threat through the letter-box expelled us, before I was one, to Daisymount Terrace, a damp and cramped addition to Gape Row, at Dundonald.
> *That* is where I began. My first clouded vision, taste and smell, was of a mound of potato farls drooling with butter, at the foot of the dozing fire, in, I believe, Mrs. Doherty's house, perhaps in the Comber Road. I also remember the smell of paraffin; or lamps I suppose. The Electric Trams ended at the Cemetery and gas was just good talk then at Dundonald.
> We graduated to gas in a Corporation house in

Wandsworth Parade. Our house was at the corner and had a generous garden. My father planted a hedge which later I clipped and cursed... I slept in the Return Room and listened to the lamplighter clanking his chain, and watched the window until the light palpitated and settled over my mantled sleep.

Granda Steel, my maternal grandfather, was short and dapper, moustached, with a bow-tie and blue eyes. He was Scottish – *Well Roybo*. He had a peppermint breath and supported a walking-cane. He took me to Smithfield where we dawdled among secondhand books...

This tantalisingly all-too-brief essay, called 'Preface to an Autosnap', suggests that McFadden has yet to fulfil himself as a prose-writer. He has in fact acknowledged that he has learnt most from prose writers: Joyce perhaps above all. This admission should cause little surprise, for McFadden's work too is manifestly autobiographical: a reading of this selection is no less than a reading of his own life. Not all of his life, perhaps, but a distillation of his imaginative experience from childhood to maturity.

Some of the early poems clearly suggest his interest in Blake, Yeats and AE. Not an unusual trio, seeing that McFadden's own family background is one of episcopalianism, unitarianism, theosophy, and agnosticism. The early religious influences have, I think, long been discarded, leaving only scepticism, in my view the most sane philosophy in this debased religious community we inhabit. So the astringent tones of scepticism, irony, wit, even of self-mocking, appear more and more in the poems of the last decade.

McFadden, perhaps the most 'rooted' of our poets, has plied his 'intricate trade' of solicitor in the heart of bomb-blasted Belfast, but the chaos of his daily experience is seldom refracted into the poetry. Here all is structured, controlled, under poetic command. Here all is disciplined into metre and counterpoint, rhyme, half-rhyme and assonance. Here all is most scrupulously channelled into organic form, concise statement, precise image.

From 1948 to 1953 McFadden co-edited *Rann,* which published work by local, English and American poets, known and unknown. In the Spring 1950 issue he wrote:

> Our roots travel widely and ignore boundaries and cultural geographical units. What we need is a way of life, personal, dignified and purposeful... Rilke's sombre reflection is painfully relevant: *You must alter your life.*

McFadden's way of life is not likely to change. It will remain private and purposeful. And his way as a poet will continue to be uniquely his own, with no concession to passing fashion, no capitulation to easy popularity, no frantic climb onto any convenient bandwagon. The way of a poet must be essentially lonely: for loneliness is the price demanded by integrity.

Throughout the winter of 1943–4, a young man of twenty-two, he wrote seven elegies in memory of his mother, recently dead:

> Now the last leaf may fall outside my heart
> That holds her beauty singing like a shell,
> The quiet voice of her that cannot die:
> The gentleness of the shy English girl
> Who married into this crazed, sterile land
> And bore a son in hope, though rifles spoke
> Against his future in the ambushed streets...

Craziness and sterility are still with us; our streets still ambushed; our lives little altered.

What can a poet do here and now but go his own way? I recall a sentence of Rilke's written during the composition of his great *Duino Elegies*:

> Art cannot be helpful through our trying to help and specially concerning ourselves with the distresses of others, but as in so far as we bear our own distresses more passionately, give, now and then, a perhaps clearer meaning to endurance, and develop for ourselves the means of expressing the suffering within us and its conquest more precisely and clearly than is possible to those who have to apply their powers to something else.

Suffering appears in many of McFadden's poems, its conquest also. Here, however, is expressed no facile optimism, no comforting sentiment. Here moods are crystallised hard. But here, too, is playfulness and the tonic joy of life. All is incantatory.

McFadden is a *living* poet with a singing voice whose work has won praise from such discriminating critics as J. Middleton Murry, C. Day Lewis, Herbert Read, Frank O'Connor. I am confident that this generous selection of his work will confirm for him his distinctive place in our tradition.

The poems assembled under the heading 'Translations and Reiterations' have been selected from the early volumes: *Three New Poets* (shared with Alex Comfort and Ian Serraillier) published by Grey Walls Press in 1942, *Swords and Ploughshares* (1943), *Flowers for a Lady* (1945) and *The Heart's Townland* (1947), all published by Routledge under the auspices of Herbert Read. The title of the section denotes that some of the early poems have been 'translated', while respecting mood and meaning, into a more laconic style. The others, 'reiterated', have been allowed to stand in their pristine innocence. 'Notes for the Hinterland' contains poems written since the publication of *A Watching Brief* (1979). 'Synge in Paris' (page 43) belongs to the Lyric Theatre. It was one of five poems read at the laying of the foundation stone by Austin Clarke on 12 June 1965. A copy of the poem with the other poems (by Padraic Colum, W.R. Rodgers, John Hewitt and Seamus Heaney) is on permanent display in the theatre. 'Irish Chippendale' and 'The lay preacher' (pages 67 and 68) are part of a sequence, 'Quaile Holdings', published in *Verifications*. *A Watching Brief* contains a related sequence, 'Immigrants', where the poem, 'The Raloo Sermon', provides a connecting link.

John Boyd

Ballyshannon

Dear Mr Allingham:
When you hear girls singing your songs,
Harping late at their spinning-wheels
These summer evenings,
Do you slacken your pace as you pass
The glancing doorways before,
Officiously,
Dusk shutters the town?

Pray, Mr Allingham:
Do you turn at the head of the town,
Stick elegant in salute,
An airy autograph,
And touch the brim of your hat;
Or do you elect to be,
Anonymously,
The singing, the song?

Translations and Reiterations

Jonathan Swift

Strolling in public gardens, he saw Death
Sidling behind the flowers, backing off
To leave life to its brief commitment, as
The branches sprang back shut on the private path.

The hollowness roared up at him from chasms.
His dreams massed in the night like refugees
Crowding the dawn's release. His daylight mind
Confronted and unmasked Death's euphemisms.

No ministering angels bent to skim
The scum of self or loosen ligatures
Of clamped horizons clotted on his mind.
The bleeding girl. The fierce erupting drum.

His huge coherence leapt from the monstrous drum,
And broke the axle of the drummer's wrists.
Below, the garden was a butterfly
Assured within the context of its dream.

Lines by Slieve Donard

The men who made these walls,
Rimming the higher ground with younger stone,
Aproned with mist or shoulder-high in sun,
Their hands absorbed and yet contemplative,
Pausing, did they lift their hands to hear
The hunted echo scurrying through the whin,
Peer for the shadow driving the stuttering sheep
Askew in flight, and the cattle lumbering
In the swollen valleys glittering with fear?

And speculate,
Above the parishes and baronies,
Picking out spires like pins and the roads' threads,
On some disaster climbing the rockface
To where their obstinate regiment of stone,
Boulder to boulder, guards the empty peak?

Dublin to Belfast: wartime

Dublin left, with its uncensored lights
Careless of retribution from the skies,
Unreprimanded and insouciant streets,
A goodnight's sleep and morning unimpaired:

You tunnel back to war, where licit light's
A swinging arm redeeming the night sky,
Grabbing for midges dancing in the dark
Over the braced and vulnerable town:

Sobered from extravagance of lights,
Adjusting to the place's temperament,
The brazen gantries and the querulous gulls
Harsh from the islands occupied by storm.

The drums

Muttering in the morning distances
Ranged as it were
Like an army under the trees awaiting command,
The live sticks talk; the monologue begins.

The drums continue through the sultry night
Tempo like leaves
Under the rain's diagonal arrowheads,
The sound tumescent in the pungent dark;

A masturbation struggling for release
Into the images it violates:
Seeking assuagement in the suppliant flags
Of white surrender stumbling through the trees.

Lines written near Downpatrick after an air-raid

Riparian fields, tidal with spring,
Daffodil-debonair clouds in a slow
Swan-processional river. Look:
Alternatively, there's moored
The island's matching miniature.

But I interpolate
A personal point of view,
Of rubble in the street
Last Easter Tuesday.

On an abandoned quay
Where barges unhumped merchandise,
The bargees loose in the town with tales
For unbelieving girls, new pennies for children,
The only pennants now
Are condescending gulls:

Where I, at my summer's edge,
Oxtered by history,
Eyes on the river's clouds, recall
How the souls of the Irish soldiery
Passed in a slow salute of geese.

Homecoming

The brittle relics did no more than claim
Tepid endorsement, for too many thumbs
Had made a guidebook out of history
And smudged the small print underneath the name.
Positioned pieces lacked the urgency
Of hate's evangelism in the drums
Ranting from windy corners back at home.
You touched your hat to plaque and monument
But kept commitment fastened like a purse
Against the famous patriot's famous tomb,
The epitaph in pet commissioned verse
That funked the warts beneath the unguent.

You need not travel to find history.
Its myths pollute the wells of the townland
And spatter maps with tribal boundaries;
And under every still or singing tree
Your recollection in tranquillity's
Of feuds obedient to a dead command.
So, tentative traveller, the journey lies
Always behind you; there's no certain track
To fullness that does not in time retreat
Back to the doors you slammed, the tugs and ties
You ran from down the liberating street,
And on yourself turned a denying back.

Prophet and loss

The preacher paused, and veered, came back to him
Corrupt, with inturned eyes and incoherent hands,
And said I am the morning, make your bed:
And he got up and stroked the fevered sheets
And coaxed the sunken pillow plump again.

You were the morning, and I was the day
That tried to hold off the implacable night.
But you remained inturned, away from me,
With deserts in your hands and journeys in your face.

Liverpool boat

Departure's in the air; and up on deck
The Old Year takes its last look at the town.
Now home is cargo, and the past's a dream
Equivocal in the night, like those gull-bright
Handkerchiefs that stammer out goodbyes.
Now home's cast off. The foam breaks in a wave,
As lights and faces tumble. On the quay
A man sings 'Auld Lang Syne' in staunch farewell;
And,
Above the exits and the entrances,
The clocktower waits for the horologer.

Elegy for a sixth-former

Collating memories of you, with your hair
Amazed like candles staggering in the air,
Big hands cut out perhaps for taming fields
Yet handy too with words, I look with a child's
Concern at the dismantling of our world,
Hearing the hiss of tiny butts you hurled
Into the simmering burn, o then, before
This surfacing delinquency of war,
Where I'm the bounder, a remove away
From your correct if tepid loyalty:
And fasten souvenirs of glance and phrase,
A jotter's sketches, while your mocking face
Obliquely glimmers from a hand-cupped flame,
Snatching a breather from a dirty game.

Paul Robeson

The summer faltering, and the town
Mending its shutters for the storms,
With glimpses through the skiffing rain
Of Donegal across the bay,
And Scotland when the early mist is blown,

I've shaped my thoughts to discipline
Nostalgic areas of the mind,
And watched a wave's imperious fin
Import white anger to the shore,
Retreat, submerge, and shoulder back again:

And, dwelling on my hankering days
When wish-world was a rockcut sea,
And poems were rushed messages
Like notes in bottles children send
Out solemnly on summer holidays,

Confident that the sea will bear
Them buoyantly to promised lands,
For some lost cause, some rightful heir –
Say that your proud dark songs have crossed
Far more than the Atlantic getting here.

Elegy for a noncombatant

1

June's like a girl out skipping in the street,
Indifferent to the bric-a-brac of war.
Disaster's still a headline, not as yet
Tanks slit-eyed in the town, boots at the door.
But o my friend
Is wheeled into a polished room to die.

Now that he has become
A leaf turned over on a calendar,
The educated conscience will require
An explanation, and a balance sheet
That tots the good days and subtracts the bad;
But what name do you give the auditor?
The young disdain us who attend their graves.

2

Death is no stranger but it brings new tears
That ridicule the clerics' promises.
Affection is an open city for
Maverick mayhem called an Act of God.
And just, as when
On the night of the first siren we glibly walked
Out from the cinema to ambushed streets
And ran like rats under the caterwaul,
So now,
I run defenceless through an abandoned dark
Subway under a no-man's-land, alone,
Seeking and fearing the ambivalent light:
Till, probating his life, unearthing cards
Postmarked with blue sea-towns, now sad ghost towns
With promenades abandoned to the sea,
I turn from picking out those journeys'-ends
Congealed in snapshots, to a close-up of
Obedient citizens wound-up for war.

Put plaster on the cut. The wound is mine;
But their infection is not my disease.
His absence clings like an amulet on my breast.

3

Hence, since remembrance probably will last
Longer than the short sum of his years,
Let me essay
To polish and keep sharp
The knives of anger, pity, vigilance.
The dead accuse us who walk on their graves.

Portrait of a poet
for William Galbraith

He culled as it were from air
Not their ghosts but smiling presences
Inhabiting gardens and strict avenues:

Reclaimed the freehold from
The limited demise; the parchment's breath
Responded to his greenfingered caress:

And when he died they found
Inside his opened body immigrant
Poems around his hospitable heart.

Elegy for a dog

This is his day; though calendars declare
That every date's an anniversary.
This is his day; the fawning sorrows creep
Back to the chair, and drown me in their eyes.
Yes I remember him, and turn away
Again as I turned homeward that sad day
His blood upon my coat and on the street,
The dogged stray of silence at my heels.

Death of a cyclist

Perhaps a girl was waiting when he was hurled
Headlong at death; wearing new gloves, a favourite scarf,
Anxious to please: anyway, part of his world
That rang its inadequate bell at the tearaway wheels.

Who, patient in rooms or crying out in the fields,
Can indicate the point where their revolution became
Charged with his demise? Round-eyed like a child's
Abandoned hoop they goggled at public blood.

And petulantly, still miles away from fear,
She tapped her foot, till rumour touched her, whispering,
Widening her suburb to a hemisphere,
Blind to the pretty pictures on her scarf.

My father had a clock

My father had a clock above the stairs.
Punctilious but benevolent, its hands
Had fingers on our pulses, in our pies;
Was like an uncle, or a grandfather
In the spare room, condoning incidents.
And then – I don't know; unaccountably –
A stranger bought it; took it in his car
To foreign parts, like Ormeau or Malone,
And I was left to climb the stairs alone.

I take the measure of my silence, but
Relapse back to a nursery of sound,
Of knitting needles ticking, or a clock
Stitching the ragged corners of the mind.
So, you who know my footstep on the stairs,
And recognise my voice across a room,
Endure the routine of my sentiment,
A sprinter coasting through pentameters,
An anarchist who packages the law;

For, out of bounds, the high-and-mighty hawk
Stands, sun in hand, biding its alien time
To swoop and sweep away our clockwork toys.

The white bird

I made a loaf of bread
And scattered it in crumbs
Under the yellowing tree,
For the white bird with the red
Beak and glittering eyes,
Who sits indifferently
Turning a confident head.

I culled old recipes
And made a loaf of bread,
And laid out crust and crumb
As bait or sacrifice.
But he humps stony wings;
Pickpocket starling come:
The quiet rat pillages.

If I could lay a hand
Upon that confident head,
And hold those glittering eyes,
And come to understand
That unrelenting beak,
I'd silence all the cries
That desolate the land.

The upland field
for John Boyd

1

Walking with the schoolmaster
About the Antrim countryside
— Lilac hills, remember me —
I bid my sentries stand aside
And let the green air fraternise
With the resistance in my mind,
The sombre look-outs in my eyes;
And tell the hedge, the tree, the field,
The ditch-flowers in the stony lane,
To conjure from the dayligone
Not just a symbol, but a sign.
Though his unspeculating mind
Is credulously sceptical,
His lumpish dicta passwords for
The village intellectual,
He's sensitive to the stylish hills,
The Mournes' perpetual marathon
From peak to corrugated shore,
Among the baronies of Down.
And I, who share his countryside,
— Leafshot roads, remember me —
Endorse his speech and silence at my side.

2

The play has changed since that first night
I argued with his obstinate gate,
And faced him in a bookish room.
The atlases are obsolete;
And cities pulled tooth after tooth
Spew their bad blood, and citizens
Expelled from sheltering parables
Follow the tracks of violence.

The boots have hammered out new moulds
From forms we counted permanent;
And now that reason holds its head
Images outface argument.
William Blake meant what he said
When he denied the world was round,
With hallelujahs in the stars
And amens on agnostic ground.
Create a world, or suffer theirs,
Quiescent in the hinterland.
The portly figure ruminates
Over autumnal rust, a hand
Chopping each punctuated phrase,
As on that summer night when death
Was still a book-word, and the wind
From Europe carried flowers in its breath.

3

I know these people, and disdain
Much that I know: the snarl of drums
Fouling an April evening;
Tight fist and tighter mouth; the slums
Of bigotry, suburban cant;
The stagnant ruts in the townland:
These were my childhood. But in time,
Though hostile, I may understand,
And retrospectively regret
A moon-meshed bridge, a crying tram,
These roads above the market town,
And call them home; for these I am.
Yet, hostile, I'll identify
With form and substance far away
From ghetto-thinking, tribal lore,
Still young enough to find a way
To the high hill that grips the sun
And holds its harvest in the hail.
So, walking with the schoolmaster
Past sights that grow more vulnerable

In the advancing night, I draw
The scene around me, naming friends
Who've fought the clockwork soldiery
And all that earns death's dividends;
– Grave-locked ones, remember me –
For the wind about the hill
Grows hoarse with voices that deny
The upland field we hope one day to till.

4

Walking with the schoolmaster
About the poignant countryside
– Violet hills, remember me –
I put my wary guard aside
And tell heart to memorialise
Pianoforte of the rain,
The cut-out shadows on the grass,
Smoke hankering from the Lisburn train;
And furbish old alliances
Between the living and the dead
– Grave-locked ones, remember me –
Against the victories ahead,
Heart's isolation and despair,
Corruption seeping into lives
Entrenched in attitudes of war,
The bandaged flags strung up again.
So, walking with the schoolmaster,
Learning by rote a countryside,
I watch and measure. Look; the stir
Of branches in the hillside field
Beckons. Silhouetted clear
Against a watercolour sun
The truthful tree stands calm and sheer
Beyond complexities of time.
I watch and measure while the sky
Accepts the night – *remember me*,
White upland field – and the last bird slips by.

First letter to an Irish novelist
for Michael McLaverty

Establishment has taken to the hills.
The capitals are bombed. But you pursue
Survival in minute particulars,
Your landscapes, intimate with sea and sky,
Perpetual, unblemished idiom
Common as dolmens and the Easter whin.

Even this city reveals dignity,
Turning a startled face from history.
If you ignore the adolescent dream,
The club-fists of the mob, the tumbled bed,
It is because, the final pattern known,
You choose the threads. And local hatreds fail
To herd your vistas to a culdesac
Or drown you in a puddle's politics.

Chance friendships are not always fortunate.
I think of someone, mutually known,
Complacent as a throstle bosoming song
Above the matchstick silhouetted town
Caught in the headlights of advancing war;
And of another portly pedant who
Talks of the revolution from a chair,
Stroking his stomach; and of that old man
Walking in mountains, gnarled with stern regret
At missing greatness (the erratic bus).

And then I think of Ireland. Of blue roads
That rivulet into Aeonic seas;
The fields bogged down with failure; the downfall
Of honest men perverted by a cause
Or dangerous verses irresponsibly
Let loose by poets and adopted by
The semi-literate candidates for power,
Or turned to dogma in schoolchildren's mouths.

Those who have lost a country, with a wound
In place of patria, can sail like winds
Among the islands and the continents,
Flying, if any, only personal flags,
Educated to brave devious seas,
Sceptical of harbours, fortunate
In being themselves, each with his personal war.

And they have charts and compasses, for some
Have made the voyage out before their time,
Confronting tempests, fangs of submarines,
Alerted to the coasts' hostility,
The accents foreign and the flags suspect.
A few received an ocean burial,
Having lost sight of continents too long,
Crazed by a magnitude of space and time,
Agnostic salt in the nostalgic wound.

We shall be wary then, and weatherwise,
Testing our strength of sail, learning the ways
Of sinuous currents singing in the rocks,
And the exotic dreams that come from thirst
And too much loneliness on the world's edge,
The midnight mutiny and the dark hold,
The shark's snarl in the wave, the loitering mines.

In time the navigator holds a course,
And heads for landfall. Yes; but, you'll observe,
The missions follow, organised with flags
And bibles for the natives. Be assured
The paths and footholds left by us will fill
With vendors of a new conformity,
Briefed by accountants. Turn to the running sea,
That carries shells like mouths to the hushed sand.

The Garryowen

The Arcadia

Old women wading, kilting skirts
Above their ivied veins, massage
Embarrassed thighs, and clumsily
Snatch water like a sign across the face.

Younger, akimbo, they were coarse
Matrons who jested while I wailed
Wet at the edge, their navy skirts
Tucked into knickerlegs or rudely held

Tumescent over fanning waves'
Screamed-at incursions: breasted-out
Like old ships' figureheads that rode
Disastrous storms they never knew about.

I chide my children to the edge,
Where faint wave shrinks from cringing toe.
They fear the claw and the quicksand,
Where I fled from the whirlpool long ago.

Glenarm
for Margaret

Nobody told me then –
When I mooned around Portrush in a wet July –
That you, thirteen, I steeped in my fourteen years,
Were in Glenarm:
Scraped girlish legs in ferns, or shrilling at sudden sea.

Who could have told me then,
Clubbing a ball uphill on the sixpenny course,
Skimming abandoned flints from the drenched strand,
Disdaining dodgem cars in the brash arcade;
Bored by the boardinghouse, restless, and pining
Beyond the gulls' tirade and the basking islands
Only a handshake over the waves' residual fuss –
That if I'd shouted, burned a derelict house,
You might have noticed; curious, come to see.

Nobody told me then –
That loneliness is rarely an only thing;
That here or there inside an expectant hand
A welcome waits for a guest or a hastening host
To explore the lines of a future etched on the palm.

How could I tell you then –
You in Glenarm, the glens spread like a palm,
Skirting the fuschias' bells, past rhododendrons and
Moonclad magnolia trees, a haze of bees –
That a boy coasting disaster, aloof on a strand,
Traced your face in the sand in hope of a quick thereafter,
To be known perhaps in a house, educated by storm,
Engrossed and busy with children singing and spelling.

Independence

The sun itself was cheering, people said;
On tiptoe in the sky, shouting hurray:
And all along the hot processional way
Laughter and songs exploded in the street
Where bombs and guns coughed blood the other day.
Dead patriots shuddered under the dancers' feet.

At last he came, his face like a black sun;
Traitor, terrorist, conspirator
Against an empire, now prime minister.
The silence hissed like rain as he stepped out
To say it to the straining faces there,
All ready to acclaim it with a shout.

But high on the draped platform he looked small,
Used up by study, exile, intrigue, jail,
Bewildered by the view inside the pale,
The final loneliness; authority
Taking his hand inside its fist of mail,
The wound and protest into custody.

And then he couldn't say it. Language failed
To mint immaculate words that could convey
A simple truth for Independence Day.
How could he say it when he *was* the thing?
He laughed out loud, and danced down like a fey
Precocious child still fond enough to sing.

Brendan Behan

The broth of an Irish boy no doubt;
But don't mistakenly neglect
The learning and the intellect,
His knowing what he was about.

He died in headlines, gratified
To find an audience in death.
The air he breathed was public breath;
His monologues were amplified.

Condemned to play the roaring-boy
Before the faceless firing-squad,
He won them over to his side
To shoot back at authority.

Some pace their lives. But he outran
Time-table and curriculum,
Leafing with an impatient thumb
Through recipes of god and man.

They'll say he failed to drown his drouth,
Like Dylan Thomas. Who's to say
What impulse prodded them to pray
At altars that required their death?

If I presume to elegise
The still sardonic skeleton,
I'll keep a record for my own,
However diffident, demise.

Roger Casement's Rising

Good Friday in good Ireland. Risen larks
Soared from his footsteps and created over
His gaunt surprise, arresting place and time,
His journey's end. And made light of the darks

And guttering private entries in his mind.
Wet primroses and primfaced violets
All-eyed his watery rising on a strand
Where shamming shells hunched from the shoreward wind.

He had no mind, smarting with salt and zeal,
For hired collectors of his private words
Indulgently put down soon to inform
And in the final judgment dock his tale.

Coy flowers, agnostic larks, ran down his fear's
Long spine of disillusion. In the end,
Disowned belongings, longings, quest undressed,
Were dirty linen, like filched souvenirs.

Sheepdog trials

Sheila and Roy and Mick: at Waterfoot
(Remember) they obeyed each whistled call,
Connived with covert signals; the pursuit
And herding-in of sheep was cunning, wise
And moving to us watching at the edge.
They won again today the paper says.
And, reading, I remember hill and hedge
Shaggy with rain, the tea and sandwiches
Sold in a corner of the barking field:
And, in the foreground, you embracing him,
The champion, who, tolerant, would yield
Neither to hand nor word, but sat erect
In solitary pride; no, pride is wrong:
In ancient loneliness; yes, gazing out
Across the sheep-pens and the fuchsia hedge,
To where the hills evaporate in cloud.

Synge in Paris
for the Lyric Theatre

On the Pont de la Concorde, between the mad
Skeltering traffic and the pampered river
Trailing a violet scarf across the town,
He eyed from a jap of shadow, his book put down,
The gurgling pleasureboat, the giggling girls
With pouting breasts and skirts fanned out like shells.
Above, the flag of France, stiff, head-in-air;
And there at his feet, twin leaves in a trance like curls.
But, unimpressed, his brooding foreign mind
Schooled by Irish drizzle, sceptical
Of total sunshine, looked for a knuckle of cloud
Over the city, leaves curling ears for the wind,
Remembering flooded fields and the smashed wall.

Folkminder

for Michael J. Murphy

That time in Cushendall
When sun tompeeped through slatted drizzle at the hills
Stretched like Pegeen Mike or Molly Bloom
Back to the tide's necklace, the wetmouthed *yes* of the sea:
Then birds flashed; and tutting hens fretted past shrunken gates.
Summer then. Yes, fuschias set their bonnets at the bees.

That summer in the Glens
When you charmed memory back to somnolent minds
Of painbright births, toil, copulation, deaths;
Exploring culverted streams, you groped for life
For love, for neverafter.

What eyes snapped then, I mind:
Your glowing kitchen and your glancing children;
Small Winifred asleep, world clutched with doll in pram:
Yourself, burdened with silence, padding roads to poach
A shadowy thought from old polluted streams;
Yourself, goodman at home, inching buckets past
Her limpid dream, her waterpale limp palm.

Night fishing

They drag the hidden net towards the shore
Nervous with shadows and attentive stones,
The village voiceless under a single star,
The sea quiescent, careless of the lines'
Whispering conversation with the shore.

The far boat creaks an oar, and a voice falls
Frail from the distance, calls, and veers to sea.
The wet lines tighten, strain; and life explodes
On to the shingle in fierce mutiny,
Riding the net in rainbow waterfalls.

Night's net hangs lightly on the countryside.
I walk back softly, with a poacher's tread,
Parting the silence, skirting the set alarms,
Around doomed dreamers scaling air to ride
Cold rainbows dying on a mountainside.

Premonition

You can never be alone again.
Here now, in the silence, you can sense
The prowling dog of loneliness slouch past
From rooms to hall, rousing a restless ring
Of questions like sloughed-off abandoned leaves.
You say lie still, or open doors to find
Always before you remonstrating eyes,
Stairways of searching feet unstitching the dark,
The heart a clock regretting its lost chime.

Second letter to an Irish novelist
for Michael McLaverty

Yourself unchanged, shy habits undisturbed:
After twenty years you still wring change
Out of the purse of knuckled prayerspent hands,
And fondle story's detail, poem's phrase,
As farmers clap a beast or rub ripe grain –
Because from ink and clabber they've come through.

Still *Sons and Lovers* you evaluate
A major novel of this century,
As when we first talked in a dying war.
But now I don't read Lawrence any more,
My favourite book a street directory
That pages streets forever running home.

How to escape from a parenthesis
Back to the narrative and argument
Is not solely a novelist's concern.
I file at words like keys that might unlock
A sentence from curt brackets' manacles,
A present tense from phrase's culdesac.

On early breathgrey mornings you walk out
And finger frost, note cuckoospit and drawn
Threads in the hedges, introverted trees:
Then, at the altar, hear unaltering word
That needs no key or confidential file,
No laddering wall or jarred heel's certainty.

I travail over clabbered clout of ground
Whose sanction's not imposed but must be worked
Up from graves with delf and bone and snarl;
And riddle shard and soil, and scrabble for
Absolving evidence of cornered gods
Thorned in the hedges, hung in decadent trees.

If, unabridged, we fish in the same stream,
You celebrate, I walk heelbrightened streets,
Squinting at dates on buildings, searching for
The architect behind a bricked-up door;
Evicted tenants in demolished streets
Who served their sentence in parenthesis.

Contemplations of Mary

1

When he said *Mary*, she did not at once
Look up to find the voice, but sat recalling
Warm patches of her childhood, and her falling
Heartoverhead in love with every glance
Of admiration crowding through the dance,
Or in the streets bent back and almost calling.

Girls put on sex like flowers; their small breasts
Emerge like blushes, knowing, innocent;
The underflow of all their ways intent
On welling up with welcome for the guests
Who darken love's white threshold. All the rest's
Above, outside, like god and government.

So she sat on when he first spoke to her.
Hearing perhaps a new sound of command,
Like parent's tug at child's reluctant hand,
Did not at once look up and answer *Sir*,
But sat with memory her conspirator,
Downcast, and did not want to understand.

But he persisted. *Mary*. She resigned
Her meadows and her rainbows to his voice,
Inevitably now, without a choice,
Surrendering all the stairways of her mind;
Then, finally bereft, was empty, blind,
Until the word bulged up and broke. *Rejoice*.

2

Then she was different. Her past perfect years
Seemed like another woman's purse, all strange
In ordinary things, keys, compact, change:
And home no longer nested up those stairs,
Involved with tables, pictures, cupboards, chairs.

Everything was leaning out askew
Since it had touched, no hardly touched her, blown
A strange breath through her branches and the mown
And planted garden of her private view,
Those yesterdays no longer *I* but *you.*

Was it her knowledge of the clouded womb
That crowded out her quiet corridors:
Her certainty of child? Or, like far doors
Slamming goodbyes, was it a shout of doom,
The dying of a world in her small room:

Her mind a skirt of fear ballooning back
To girlish unencumbered days when life
Required no definitions; sweetheart, wife
Made love, embroidered, lived without some lack
Of meaning like a rat at every crack:

Mary, still girl enough to twirl her hood
From birth and death conspiring in her blood
Against the bright truth of her platitude?

3

After the dying, tidying her room,
She pondered, wondered why he had cried out
In protest for his father. Was his shout
Indictment of the seed that filled her womb
Or plea for some known name to mark his tomb?
Now she was parched and hollowed out with doubt.

She had been satisfied the way things were,
Girl among girls, doing the usual things.
Then she had been exalted, hearing wings
Applauding through the galleries of air;
Came to know words that first had made her stare,
And talk to common people as to kings.

It never was her doing. She had been
Only the bottle for the conjured wine.

Involved with something magic or divine,
She had no axe to grind, no slate to clean,
Had never bothered with a party line.
Most of the things he said she did not mean.

Now she was empty. The last drop had gone,
And she was her own Mary, uninvolved
With parables or politics, resolved
To self, undedicated, pledged to none.
And just before the colours blurred, dissolved,
She closed the door on her disfigured son.

4

I am the breath that stirred
Your bells to jubilance;
Conjured from cold distance
As surely as a bird
Immense obeisance:
I am the word.

My irresponsible
Dialogue broke down,
Was hooted, hissed and blown
Off stage in ridicule,
My sad forgiving clown
A love-crossed fool.

But I would blow again
My horn into your sleep;
Herd rational thought like sheep
Into a nursery pen;
Scatter my wolves to sweep
Doubt from the plain.

Yes, I would fill your page,
Your lines with poetry:
With liberating key
Empty the clipped lark's cage,

*And give back wings to free
Ecstatic rage.*

*Mary, I am cold,
Bare on the brink of mind.
Open, and let me find
A place to grip and hold,
To thrust the exiled seed
In knowing mould.*

The Garryowen

A Soldier's Song; the silence: then the roar
Of Lansdowne-Irish voices. (Who reflects
On Morgan, Cromey, Bailey, Moran, Kyle,
And Sammy Walker and Blair Mayne? The score
Will be forgotten in a little while.)
Stopped on the line, O'Reilly genuflects.

The scrummage labours over seminal ground,
While fledgling wings hang loosely for a sign.
Ecstatically, the undulating crowd
Climbs to a climax, tolerates the wound;
Implores, deplores, ejaculates aloud.
On, up and under, forwards; charge the line.

Irish for an afternoon, they wait
For gory glory-o, the faceless men,
Close men from Belfast, Ballymena, loud
As uncorked Dubliners, and imprecate
Together in some sort of brotherhood.
Mothproofed, the old myths stagger out again.

The ball hangs like a sighted bird, and falls.
Lost causes rally on the emerald grass.
While clockfaced Fate knits destinies from time,
Who looks through game to life; hears ashblown calls:
Sees shamrock-favours bloom to climbing clouds
Above the cancelled world that missed the pass?

The symbols dominate and germinate.
Ball shamrocks like a bomb; the partisan
Applause gasps like the last transparent brick.
But mention also, in italics quote,
The language that survives the rhetoric,
Kyle's poetry of movement, his *élan*.

The barking journalists lift pints and vet
Form and performances. In Davy Byrne's
The Belfast men with club conformist ties
Buy quick ones, nationality, and rate
Moffett and Mulligan, drop-kicks and tries.
Short of the line, an offside bomber turns.

Let's talk of Championship and Triple Crown,
But not forget in toasting victory
What the final shout will be about.
Before you put the sporting record down,
Ponder an Irish remedy for rout:
The Garryowen, and the game set free.

Verifications

March

Stoned cheek turned again
The stone turned from the tomb:
Unvault spring
Like a lad,
For your parish needs hoeing
And a weeding of snakes
In constricted ground.

Aghast with ghosts in houses
Mothers and children stay
Tears for another day,
Since a corpse provided
Everyday.

Hold up your favour Patrick
Not like a riot-shield
Or clerics with their bibles
Or perpetrators' hands
Guilty of blood on the tarmac
Vengeance on old sick walls.

From Downpatrick Cathedral
(Abashed by daffodils)
Pronounce a curse on reptiles
Fused to ejaculate;

From Downpatrick Cathedral
(Three saints smudged on a wall)
Now that Easter flusters
From the shattered egg

Stained window-glass and rubble,
Chance another spring;
With hailstones maybe,
Or perhaps daffodils.

Keeping my place

1

In fortunate places
They worry only
About a prospect of rain –
Who's for tennis
Deckchairs and parasols
Shopping without
Barriers soldiers saracens
The person touched by strangers;
War conditions with
The enemy inside–:
What private hate
Wrecked the Abercorn;
What spurious hand
Gutted Smithfield?

2

In a wet jilting June
I review and assess
What I have made of half
A century, and guess
With trepidation what
I'll do with a bonus of years,
A post-dated cheque
To be marked invalid perhaps
By a bilking bank.

3

I began in violence and
My age now coincides
With hooded murder and
My children know no other
Place or style
Than the bomb the fist and thugs'

Intimidation,
The tortured corpse in the ditch.

4

The toad puffs and the snake smiles;
Cancelled faces kill.
I recall two figures poised
Between the sea and the shore
On the fringe of life,
In my early fatherhood;
Yes they
Had time and place to affirm
Or to be nonchalant,
To whom I sang old songs
Driving the car
Through strange townlands.

5

The toad bellows and the snake snarls.
Songs suspect now, the younger ones
Have seldom grasped
Bucket and spade without blood
Coursing like sea
From the Irish curse that wrecked
Picnics and politics –
(Mitchel and Yeats; their cry:
War in our time O Lord).
May peace, I taught them to pray
From the Upanishads,
May peace and peace and peace
Be everywhere.

6

I declare
That in this vicious town
Whose future drips on a line
Unhoused from the weather,

Where masked men celebrate
Cudgel and petrol-bomb –
That along High Street
A river used to stride
Sails lintel-high in the air,
A semaphore:
Now culverted underground.
Expatriate now, I look
At the trees my father made;
Stateless, I look around
At the loss and the waste,
The desolate acres; and watch
My children stooping to lick
And stick down emigrants' labels.

Kew Gardens

Queuing in Kew Gardens
For tea and sandwiches –
The English take for granted
Where we take liberties –
We trespassed upon sunlight
And unfunereal flowers,
And no one thought to ask us
To prove our names were ours.
Unbroken glass in windows
Reflected as we crossed,
And the present had a future
Uncorrupted by the past;
For children ran and shouted
Against a bantering breeze,
Without a glint of murder
In an innocence of trees.

Suffering English tea as
A chaser to the bread,
I swapped with a German widow
Our blitz for her air-raid;
Said sunshine made us anxious
Like streetlamps in the war
In Dublin, while in Belfast
The dark went on as far
As the hills till the last siren
Straightened to All-Clear,
And the kettle and the tea-cups
Domesticated fear.

Edwardian sunlight failing,
Like imperial grace,
On an afternoon of tea-cups,
I chose to reminisce
On similar bombs and sirens,
Families under the stairs,

Rats blazing from the manholes,
The Spitfires and Messers;
On bankruptcy of empire
And fraud of nationhood:
Then framed an awkward handshake
For all I'd left unsaid.

For I hadn't marred our wartime
Reminiscences
With a provincial quarrel
Remote beyond the trees;
Or complicated tea-time
With cocktail theory
That Belfast was in labour
Over identity.
The killer wears a mask, and
The victim gives his name
To just another headstone;
The clichés stay the same.

The waitress hurried on to
Set another place;
And the children ran and shouted
Against the bantering breeze.

Daisymount Terrace

1

From the school in the Church Quarter
Lately laden with books and tasks
My brother whooped downhill,
Fighting allcomers, back
To paraffin lamps and griddle bread
The Moat and the Church overhead,
And the Reverend Cottar poised
Pruning his sermon; where
The stream behind the houses stole
Pebbling his sleep.

Then Daisymount Terrace
Was beyond the tramlines
And the festering city's war,
And himself with his popgun lost
Between the opposing armies –
Where the stream had no name,
But collogued with children among
The humpedup fields

And the cottages,
Gape Row limewashed, the gardens
Hunching up to the Moat:
For twisted kitchen-spoons
To ferret for giants' bones;
Dundonald a dream between
Ghetto's eviction and
The virgin house with the garden
Cultivated and groomed,
Outpost in a violent land,
By our father making our world.

2

Gardening I look at my hands
Veined like his the stream
Still stumbling unnamed,
And myself also aghast
Between the opposing armies –
Slow to pluck weeds –
And Daisymount Terrace now
Lacks fields for a daisychain
For a mayor in a frightened town.

The stream trembles unnamed
And a tithe
Of the Church Quarter
Enfolds the school, while I
Stammer downhill lacking
A shout from my brother
His keeper and sleeper
His brother grown in his place
With a father's hands and stance
In recovered forgotten ground.

3

With nettles in my hands
In an innocent afternoon,
My brother running back,
With whose guilt in my hands
The stream a gutter now –
Silenced by traffic ground
To a redhanded stop
A rumour of bombs –
I listen hand at ear
For a mercy of water and
My brother's confident shout
In an innocent afternoon.

Irish Chippendale

From the unitarian churchyard,
Dove-tailed in their vault,
Those ancient cabinet-makers
Devised the way he built.

Jealous administrator
Of family estate,
He banned his sister's love-talk
With the clerk in New Bridge Street.

He jostled the process servers
Spinning a coin for the brief,
And sent in word to the lawyer:
Quail of Irish Street.

From that girl's disaffection
My father got his name,
And his son never fashioned
Irish Chippendale.

The lay preacher

Coming in by the bridge they scanned
The incestuous parish, noting beyond
The comfortable fields, withdrawn
Tête-à-tête of trees and the pet
Domestic hills, the muscular
River's curved maternal arm
Jealous and threatening like a wing.

His sermon manifested more
Than similes and parables,
The scanty text a pretext for
Bold metaphors and miracles.
But the girl sat listening to the bees'
Muted organ music, while
Concurring breezes turned the leaves.

Smiles and hands in the porch; the trap
Glittering at the gate. The girl,
Holding his strap of books, moved on
Tolerant of involved goodbyes,
Sunlight catching the brooch at her throat,
And strayed to a family vault, to spell
Out names that segregated death.
Then his step quickened, came at last.

Quails in their wood; and up on the hill,
Aloof in episcopalian ground,
The lone invader of their blood
Lay without their name or his.
But she composed her gloves and hair
As the trap flashed past the river's breeze,
Unaware that the man on the hill
Had left his blood for her quickening.

Tuesday

The shawlie always came on Tuesday
With a beaten smile and her child
And ate her dinner on the doorstep
Off an old Sunday plate my mother served —

I met her once elsewhere
In another street,
And tilting schoolcap said
How-do-you-do-hallo —

And she
Shawled her child and wept
In Aston Gardens

A Watching Brief

Out in the country

Out in the country
Was beyond the seventh green,
Where the villas,
Trailing behind, let fields
Run on to ruminate
Across the promising fairways.

Surprising mornings —
When, wakened by banding birds
Terse, xylophonic;
School shelved with the bawdied books;
You railed the curtain back
To a new beginning —

Beckoned and chivvied
Over the new-pin grass,
Beyond a scotched mist
Soberly edging
Into a reticent haze,
Day's acquiescence:

Till, on the seventh
Dew-coruscating green,
Without forewarning,
The sun appeared pin-high
From over the stymie trees,
On the top of the morning.

It didn't matter
That no dog-walker saw
Mashie and putter
Iron out the bunkered fault;
Your run of birdies, or
That fabulous eagle.

For you played solo;
Partnered only by
A caddying silence
Attending on your game,
And following a style
That took your meaning.

Overtime

Pharmaceutical antiquity,
Fumed oak and bevelled glass;
Brass plates with Latin sobriquets,
Framed letters on display;
A sallow sink in the dispensary:

And out in the disintegrating yard,
Behind abandoned plants,
Milk-bottles' collarettes of curd,
The roof-drip's rusty beard,
An outhouse with an eyepatch window-board.

Over the years, he reckoned, he'd put down
A hundred, give or take;
And shrugged off any sense of sin
Merely for having been
A catspaw for some long-armed citizen.

But when the old tom broke the system, and,
Catapulting free,
Hissed acid from the bottle-stand,
His sure, professional hand,
Reneging, lifted sentence with the blind.

Self-generation

But none of them can sing, McKelvey said;
And revelation's not
A pedantry of detail, but
A quasi-resurrection of the dead,
An orphic note.

The things I dig, he said fastidiously,
Are seldom if at all
Agri- or horti- cultural;
Raked midden heaps of corned mythology,
Or cloacal.

Their singular self-esteem, he said, aggrieved,
Upstages poetry
With cult of personality;
The nipple-greed to be the best-beloved,
Exclusively.

Observe the banjos tighten, he enjoined,
In preparation for
The next award or sinecure.
Sold out at festival and one-night stand,
The self's a whore.

Allotments

Between the wars,
On the fringes of the town,
Ex-servicemen and jobless artisans
Salvaged and tilled,
Stanzaically, inhospitable ground;

Where bicycles,
Heavy as mangles, propped
Against a lean-to, sported lemonade
Bottles, strapped,
Each white or amber with its milk or tea.

On their hillsides,
Wavering in the sun
Of a shimmering afternoon, or clipped alert
In early frost,
The shadows semaphored back to the town

Whose animal crawl
Threatened their purview.
But, with the war, the villas stopped; cement
Mixers grew
Statuesque, like mines from the Great War.

Then spades became
Weapons for victory;
To dig was just as blessed as to kill:
The system claimed
Back as its own the outposts on the hill.

After the war,
The guns and spades were stored
In mouldering churches, and the mixers churned
Out citizens
With garages, whom no one semaphored.

Armistice Day 1938

Every year in the Assembly Hall
We would exhume the dead
Protagonists of the Great War.
With marbled eyes McKelvey prayed
For unknown uncles killed at Passchendaele.

The blood-roll of the drums, the bugle's cry,
The curt succeeding hush
For masochistic memory,
Insinuated a death-wish;
And history sugared to mythology.

In my last year, the radio relayed
A nation's fading grief
Live from the London Cenotaph;
But my suspended disbelief
Was shattered with the silence when a loud

Dissident voice charged puppet-masters with
Rigging another war.
McKelvey broke ranks also, and
Rejected bloody murder for
Conflicting medals masking the same cloth.

Sound sense

Lucas used to gloss his party piece,
MacDiarmid's *Watergaw*,
By stressing how *its chitterin' licht*
Conveyed the stuttering flight
Of water fowl skimming a river's breeze:

Till finally a plastic Scot complained;
Translated *Rainbow*. But
He hardly faltered in defence;
Just veered, and took his stance
On sound suggesting more than language meant.

M'Ilhagga raised his somnolent head,
Insulted back to life,
Bitter from years of reading and
The will to comprehend.
Tit, fart and willy were the words he said.

Notes for the Hinterland

Post-war

Cold and clear are the words
That belong to bright March days,
If you think of mornings
When sky is gunmetal blue
And a terse breeze flexes its strength in the raw trees.

The hard years after the war
When life, in a word, was spare,
Were like March mornings
Cold-shouldered or cut by spring,
Yet with promise, in spite of the promises, sharpening the air.

Remembered merchandise –
Shelved childhood's packets and tins –
Trailed back from limbo,
Nostalgically labelled, and we
Reflected on pots and pans, matched saucers and spoons.

Under the cenotaphs
The poppies foundered on stone;
And over the bomb-holes
Pert window-boxes presumed.
They restored the excursion train and the ice-cream cone.

Then we dallied with summer again,
Making light of the buried bombs,
The snarled wire's venom,
The abandoned towers on the dunes;
And salvaged stray bullets for girls to give to their sons.

The Grand Central Hotel
for Robert Greacen

1

      In June, examiners
      Seconded from
The London Guildhall School
Of Music (Speech and Drama) commandeered
      The Londonderry Room,
And summoned elocution-anglicised
Provincials to pout London vowel-sounds;
      Posed as it were
      For kiss or medicine:

      Where, testily carpeted,
      They diffidently
Surrendered up their lines,
Still fighting shy of their stepmother tongue;
      While, down-to-earth, below,
Incorrigibly aboriginal,
The page-boy squired his privileged reserve,
      Between the lift
      And the revolving door.

2

When officers and their whores,
Hotfoot for the hotel,
Forced you back to the gutter's lip,
You reckoned them as war's
Recruitment of the rubbish-tip,
And counted your contempt contemptible;

When, out of character,
You threw off diffidence,
And remonstrated in the street
Against the abattoir,

The flatulent bellow and the bleat
Of butcher's meat dressed up as citizens;

Reluctant activist:
What forced you to declare
Your singlemindedness before
A crowd you still mistrust?
It wasn't love. No; rather more
Distaste, and loyalty, and being there.

3

Those were the palmy days when affluence,
    With cash in hand,
Benevolently knocked at doors,
    A Fyffe-banana man,
Paid to give money to the provident.

Swanning in taxis past the river's sleep,
    Or rakishly
Riding the Jaguar, we lived
    It up, you should observe,
In gracious living as distinct from Life.

Upholstered corners intimate with drink's
    Complicity,
A world in a glimmering glass, to be sipped
    In purchased elegance,
A world away from the world and the shout in the street:

Where dainty legs and unembarrassed eyes,
    The delicate tilt
Of cigarette red from the lips,
    Concealed in masquerade
The idiomatic hatred of their streets.

4

This is hostile territory now.
In Royal Avenue

Planners and bombers have united to
Wreck or eliminate
Taken-for-granted, only-to-be missed
Familiar presences.
You miss the water when the well runs dry.

Here, where a millionaire
Hoovered the street at midnight, choked with sin,
God's drunken seneschal,
You ranged the library, stalked titles down
At Greer's in Gresham Street,
And through the lanes past where the stony head
Hangs, lidless, lintel-high.

Those boarded windows displayed waxwork boys
In blazer, cap and tie,
Models of uniform propriety,
Observed on Saturdays
When you descended on the bandying town
With florin or half-crown
Warm as a girl's hand urgent on the thigh.

And later, in the war,
When poets patronised the lavatory
Inside the grand hotel,
Disdaining public inconveniences,
We gravely buttonholed
With foyer-chat persons of consequence,
As if habitués there.

This hostile territory's symbolised
By the bricked-up hotel
Inside a cage to keep the bombers out,
Where soldiers document
The dirty tricks of violence, and you
From time to time attend
For leave to motor through Victoria Square.

Conveyancer

      I remember your saying
      That among our acquaintances
      There was scarcely a reader who
Was not ambitiously, however covertly,
      A writer also; who
Read just for love without a vested interest too.

      I omitted to mention
      The withdrawn conveyancer
      Who, throughout my apprentice years,
Taciturn in his tent of blue tobacco smoke,
      Probed at ancient roots
Of title in shrinking lease and wizened fee farm grant.

      Compulsively weeding
      Through recitals and convenants,
      He examined the drift of a field
Towards a ramification of streets and sites with red boundaries,
      Down to the last demise,
Where a brisker narration begins new chapters of lives and deaths.

      You could say it was factual,
      A sort of biography
      Of properties shaping a town;
And their people coming and going, appurtenant, in a word,
      Till they claimed the ultimate word,
Unanswerable at the end, in the form of the probated will.

      Or again, alternatively,
      That his reading was really romance;
      For the parchment pages proclaim
A myth of ownership for ever-and-a-day,
      Whose hereditaments
Are sanctioned by yellowing skin mortgaged to truculent time.

Mortgage redemptions

Reserving judgment, let us say
The middle years
Like Common Law enchanced by precedent,
Preserve the freehold of forgotten fields,
Riparian memories of the culverted stream,
A perpetuity
Of springtime that outlasts each transient spring.

The parchment leases you prepared
At twenty-two,
Now, with the loans repaid, the sub-demise
Redeemed, revert to your remembering hands,
Your naive signature
A wide-eyed witness to the act and deed.

Lessees return, and look at you
Inquiringly,
Their families reared, sophisticated to
New styles and appetites and ennuis:
Compare their wounds, or credit-worthiness,
With yours; and smile
Acknowledgment that you have made it too.

They talk of semi-villas, rates,
Adopted roads,
Techniques of gardening and the pampered car;
Insurances, and then, perhaps, a will:
And sometimes, moved to impropriety,
Cough, and recall
Summers before the builder slew the trees.

Sancto's dog

1

Come to the door,
Miss Anderson, with the lapdog slavering
Concern against your pinafore.
Listen for archers' bows in Stringer's Field.

Wait.

Call home your dog,
Sancto, the black Alsatian, silently
Skirting the children's frozen games,
The yellow eyes reserved for harder things.

Wait.

Joan Hamilton,
Run in your party frock with flying tails,
Hide in the entry from the kiss;
Fondle your hair back to its Sunday slide.

Wait.

Miss Pinkerton,
Mouth tight with pins, a needle on your breast,
Your pince-nez screwing towards the light,
Wear out your heart upon another's sleeve.

Wait.

You, redhaired maid
In the house in the culdesac, eavesdropping on dreams,
Coax him to talk in his sleep of girls
High-heeled in the evenings, dangerous in silk.

Wait

2

Still in the family way,
The houses suffer life.
But alien tenants glance from windows, or
Usurp the trimmed prim privet's privacy.
The streets, the same,
Are taken over by exorbitant cars.
Just coteries
Of grown-up trees, prehensile, recollect,
Indeed encapsulate,
The cornered field before
They folded it and carried it away,
With all the picnic things
Of childhood, adolescence; yesterday.

Wait.

3

Startled, you say hallo
To Mrs Robinson
Contending with the grass,
Say *All this time*;
And cautiously unflap the past,
Potentially a letter-bomb
Whose sealed constituents on release
Unite to maim.

And then, uneasily,
You falter and suspect,
And then become aware,
That she is not
The mother but the daughter, who's
Mistaken you (so like him) for
Your father; and you say your name,
With mild regret.

Wait.

4

You, redhaired maid,
A fact of life still unmythologised,
Another listener minds the dreams
You flirted with beside the moonlit bed:
Calls Sancto's dog
To pad the pavements to the light's arcade,
Where, silhouetted, he informs
The absences of their identical lives.

Wait.

5

It must have been
Before the hedge was grown, because,
Small as you were
And cautioned to stay put,
Nothing obscured your anguish from the street.

Wait.

Hand on the door
Of the anonymous car, its strange
Driver alert,
She called anxiety
And reassurance, but still made to go.

Wait.

O where was *Vote*?
You were too small to follow. She
Would disappear
Round nameless corners, and
You'd stand for ever, holding a laurel's hand.

Time's present

I promised you I'd buy
A silk dress and a box
Of King George chocolates
Embossed with his golden head.
My father told me how,
At the tobacconist's,
Rutherford Mayne threw down
His first week's sovereign
And named the dearer blend.
But I'd no chance to pay
Out of my bright new pounds
My grown-up compliment;
My father bought the flowers
We laid upon your grave.
Time past's time's present now.
The sleek dress and the box
Of gorgeous chocolates,
Shelved in the gloryhole
Of broken promises,
Acquire, interpolate,
Though self-bespoken now,
New, mythic presences.

Helston

i.m. James Thompson McFadden

Some wait. Some travel distances.
But *it* is never late; it is you
Who one day will be late of where you are.

Imagine next year's Floral Dance
With only the ashes of his company,
The burnt-out hospitality of his hearth.

But now, with a seemly stateliness,
His body lies on a shrouded bed,
Intent upon itself, careless of life:

And yet, with a curious courtesy,
Tolerant of their plans, resigned
To wait for the conclusions of their love.

After the broadcast

Uncertain of your timing, you
Kick at the final paragraph,
    The margins streaming
Like lane-tapes signalling
The clock adjudicating on the wall.

Then, ventriloquial, overhead,
Official voices tidy up
    The wavelength for
Big Ben's sonority;
Father of millions, bursting with the news.

The man behind the window thumbs
Approval, or at least reprieve;
    And, tension broken,
The studio unwinds,
Unflapping pockets, cigarettes and words.

The lifeless microphone's ignored
By voices it materialised;
    No longer focus
For speech and acting eye,
Invigilator of page-hushing hand.

Outside, bland traffic in the street
Insinuates that no one stayed
    At home to listen.
Your unprojected voice
Sticks in your throat; the number's still engaged.

Maryville Street

These little palaces,
Doomed in a street of executioners,
Perpetuate,
With yellowing facing-brick
Gracing the exits and the entrances,
Remembered terraces
In hinterlands, before the pestilence.

Diverted by patriots' bombs,
The brusque car frets and simmers to a halt;
And you, perforce,
Study and learn by heart
A two-up and two-down, the trite
Delph at the window, while
You pare in your mind indifferent fingernails:

Till, loose in the captive street,
She scrambles like a frightened fugitive,
Not *to* but *from*.
Rejecting a questioning hand,
Cries out abandonedly *She's gone!*
Horror rather than grief
Weals in her wake as she makes for the sealed-off town.

Sketches of Boz

1 *The blacking factory*

On his twelfth birthday,
Quick, eager and delicate,
He was sold to a rotting house
At Hungerford Stairs.
In the cellars, garbage rats
Plundered, and spat decay.
This, he had heard them say,
Was to be his station in life.
The birthday boy
Prayed to blow out the present like candlelight.

On later birthdays,
Famous, caressed and proud,
After the greetings and gifts,
The kisses and smiles,
Gargantuan dinners with friends,
Fierce walks through the bootblack streets,
He would sit in his room alone
And, pale in the candlelight,
Listen again
To the dungeon under the boards of his carpeted mind.

2 *The appraisal*

His father swore,
Addicted to debt like drink,
That all his goods, wherever situate,
Of what
Ever nature or kind,
Did not,
Vested or in contingency,
Exceed in their totality ten pounds.

The Appraiser viewed
A youngster, steadying fear

With dignity, exhibit stoically,
Perforce,
Meagre habiliments:
Wrote off
Their shrunken value, and ignored
The ancient watch precociously chained to his heart.

3   *Ellis & Blackmore*

Small for fifteen,
He wore his soldier-cap askew,
Assertively, and
Was eager for words, a scavenger
Among the alleyways
Of badinage and repartee,
A connoisseur of unbelievable names.

Up at his desk,
Fingering out like braille the carved
Initials of boys
Of earlier tenure, scheduling documents
Red-ribboned for the courts,
He'd pilfer an expensive phrase
From pompous parchments and sententious wills.

Identified –
The boy from Ellis's – he had,
Professionally,
Access to famous names, a right
Of way to privacies
Behind the postures and parade.
He infiltrated, scribbling on his palm.

His clients were
Characters with impediments,
Eccentrically
Knotted and private; yet obliged,
Language's litigants,
To remonstrate. He covertly
Ran to the stairhead, dusted the office chair.

4 *Hungerford Market*

Dandified gallery-man,
He straddled and upstaged
Hungerford Market; aired
Success like a cravat;

While, features varicosed
And ridiculed by sweat,
A toiling journeyman
Shouldered a somnolent child.

Recalled from truancy
By the backward-looking boy's
Somnambulistic stare,
Young Boz bought cherries; and,

Ambition's appetite
Nailed back to the bare board,
Extravagantly fed
The unrelenting mouth:

While the father, bent with his load,
Eyes lashed to the dragging street,
Tholed grit assaulting his throat
And the cobbles shipwrecking his feet.

5 *Mary Hogarth*

Perhaps, noting her bosom's hint
Of womanhood, the tilt-of-her-head's implied
Assertion of self, he feared
The morning when she'd come down
And fail to recognise him; pass
The paper and the time of day
With language alien to their intimacy.

Affronted by her naive death,
The bluff perhaps of his equivocal
Ménage à trois, in a phrase,

Abruptly called, he put on
Her ring proprietorially.
Young, beautiful, and good, he said:
At seventeen, immaculately dead.

Her ring, *his* now, the symbol of
An otherworldly bigamy that made
The best of both worlds, grew
Endearing on his hand;
And he could openly refer
To his undying love, acclaim
His angel, without compromising fame.

6   *48 Doughty Street*

    Surprisingly,
The first-to-be-told, the famous Gad's Hill desk
    Is just a chattel, stained
And grained with blots of discarded, overspilled words:

    While, curiously,
The public reading-desk, his one-night stand,
    Though cornered, winded and worn,
Has him up reading fiercely through the halls.

Young, confident and flash in Doughty Street –
    Doughty indeed –
Signing the lease he hungered for
The freehold to redeem the Marshalsea.

Not yet a mortgagor to affluence,
    He boyishly
Breezed through these rooms, impatiently
Straightening the curtains, stirring up the fire.

    Then, hastily,
He made his move before the lease ran out,
    Success, security,
Pursued by the Appraiser at the door.

7 Maria Beadnell

She brought it on herself
Writing out of the blue,
Chancing her arm; and he,
Enraptured, no less culpable,
Was not slow to embrace
The chance to make the fiction actual.

He had transmogrified
His love and her disdain
Into a masterpiece;
Had locked her fast in literature.
Then, not unnaturally,
He fell in love with what he'd made of her.

But when she took his hand,
Silly in middle-age,
He fumbled for his pen,
The acid for the caricature;
And, passion petrified,
Ushered her back again to literature.

8 Miss Ellen

Miscellanies
Of True Romances tell how Older Men,
Bored by their wives, pursue
Trite slips of girls. There's no
Fool like an old fool; mutton feigning lamb.

Nevertheless,
They're not just armchair lovers, for if they
Abandon dignity,
They quicken step and glance,
Brush up their smiles and titivate their dress.

Inimitable?
His story was the same, and not his best.
Like them, he falsified

The books of middle-age;
Cooked-up a lyric from the turgid prose.

They say that she
Dissembled at first; but who can counsel how
A small-part player should
Perform when beckoned out
To play the lead in a Great Man's Amour?

If she had said:
*What do you want; what can I add to your
Understanding of life?*
He might have said: *Yourself.*
More poignantly, perhaps: *Your ignorance.*

9   *The public readings*

You will remember how he made a fire
Of all the correspondence from the past;
And how, irreverently,
The children roasted onions in the ash.
The wife by then
Had been discarded. Soon the boys would go.
Only the dear girls stayed, like furniture.

And how he worked to prise the characters
Free from the burden of the narrative;
And then promoted them
Into a one-man travelling puppet-show,
With all the strings
Tied to his fingers, or like a lasso
To rope in and corral the wild applause.

And how, actor manqué, he played the parts —
Exclusively, since he'd created them —
Of wry and passionate souls
Swarming and squandering in his halflit streets
And tenements;
And how, as author, he took curtain-calls,

And, solo, finger-blew the actor's kiss:

And, reckless of advice, plunged deeper in
The fog that made illusion credible;
Until, with *Oliver*,
He acted murder as reality.
The doctors marked
The rising tide of his abandonment
Menacing moorings and decaying wharves.

Infatuated with an audience
He'd made from lust for love: seduced, he craved
Uncritical love for *him*
Rather than for the semblances of art;
Distracted from
The solitary confinement in his heart
Of the abandoned, unforgiving boy.

Bibliography

Russian Summer (Gayfield, Dublin: 1941)
Three New Poets, with Alex Comfort and Ian Serraillier (Grey Walls Press, Billericay, Essex: 1942)
Swords and Ploughshares (Routledge, London: 1943)
Flowers for a Lady (Routledge, London: 1945)
The Heart's Townland (Routledge, London: 1947)
Elegy for the Dead of The Princess Victoria (Lisnagarvey Press, Lisburn: 1953)
The Garryowen (Chatto and Windus, London: 1971)
Verifications (Blackstaff Press, Belfast: 1977)
A Watching Brief (Blackstaff Press, Belfast: 1979)

As editor:
   with Robert Greacen, *Ulster Voices* (Ulster Voices Publications, Belfast: 1943)
   with Robert Greacen, *Irish Voices* (Belfast: 1943)
   with Barbara Hunter, *Rann* (Lisnagarvey Press, Lisburn: 1948–53)